Mediterranean Salads

Don't miss This Collection of Mediterranean Fresh Salads to Keep Healthy with Taste

Valerie Reynols

By reading this document, the reader agrees that under no circumstances is the author responsible for any losses, direct or indirect, which are incurred as a result of the use of information contained within this document, including, but not limited to, — errors, omissions, or inaccuracies.

Table of Contents

Mediterranean cobb salad

The Mediterranean cobb salad are classic diet, mainly when there is a flair added to it. The ingredients and instruction are listed below.

Ingredients

- ½ cup of sour cream or plain yogurt
- ¼ cup of milk
- 1 package of falafel mix (6 ounces)
- ¼ cup of chopped seeded peeled cucumber
- ½ cup of pitted finely chopped Greek olives
- 8 cups of bacon strips, cooked and crumbled
- 2 medium sized finely seeded and chopped tomatoes
- 1 medium ripe peeled and chopped avocado
- 3 hard boiled large chopped eggs
- 4 cups of baby spinach
- 4 cups of torn romaine
- ¼ teaspoon of salt
- 1 teaspoon of minced parsley

Directions

- Cook the falafel depending on the manufacturer's Directions.
- Let it cool off
- Crumble and or coarsely chop falafel
- Combine the sour cream, cucumber, parsley, salt and milk in a small bowl
- In a separate larger bowl, combine spinach and romaine.
- Transfer to a platter
- Organize the crumbled falafel and the remaining ingredients over greens
- Drizzle with dressing ready for serving

Nectarine and beet salad

This recipe makes a scrumptious inclusion to variety of mixed greens mainly with the beets, nectarines and feta cheese. The choice of ingredients may not reflect your favorite salad but that is a lie of one's eyes. This salad can become your favorite choice for a home salad.

Ingredients

- ½ cup of crumbled feta cheese
- ½ of medium sized sliced nectarines
- 1 can of sliced drained beets (14 – ½ ounces)
- 2 packages of spring greens mixed salad (5 ounces each)
- ½ cup of balsamic vinaigrette

Directions

- Toss all greens in a serving dish with nectarine and vinaigrette
- Top with cheese and the beets
- Serve immediately for a better taste

Balsamic cucumber salad

Cucumber is a perfect healthy salad for variety of dishes especially for kabobs, chicken and or anything hot off the grill. The Directions and directions are shown below.

Ingredients

- ½ cup of balsamic vinaigrette
- 1 medium halved and thinly sliced red onions
- 1 large halved and sliced cucumber
- 2 cups of grape tomatoes cut into half

Directions

- Combine the tomatoes, onions, cucumber in a large bowl
- Introduce vinaigrette then toss to coat.
- Refrigerate when it is cover until serving
- Stir in the cheese and then serve with a slotted spoon
- Enjoy

Tzatziki shrimp cucumber rounds

Ingredients

- 2 tablespoons of finely chopped peeled cucumber
- 2 medium size cucumbers slices cut into ¼ -in
- 1.4 cup of reduced fat plain yogurt
- 1/8 teaspoon of garlic salt
- 6 bacon strips
- 1/8 teaspoon of dill weed
- 1 or 2 tablespoons of canola oil
- 24 shrimp peeled and deveined (32 – 40 pound)

Instruction

- Combine the yogurt, garlic salt, dill and chopped cucumber to set aside in a small bowl.
- Lengthwise and widthwise, evenly cut each bacon in halves.
- Using the bacon, wrap each piece of shrimp and lock them with a toothpick.
- In a larger nonstick skillet, heat the oil with medium temperature.

- Cook the shrimp in manageable batches for 3 – 4 minutes on every side until crispy
- Spoon the yogurt sauce on each cucumber slice.
- Top with the shrimp
- Serve and enjoy

Tomato feta salad

This recipe is perfect for balsamic dressing. It can be topped and served with a variety of dishes or even combined with other veggies to quench the appetite for fresh healthy vegetables. Below are the ingredients and Directions.

Ingredients

- 2 tablespoons of balsamic vinegar
- ¼ cup of crumbles feta cheese
- 1 – ¼ teaspoon of minced basil (fresh or dried)
- ½ teaspoon of salt
- ½ cup of coarsely chopped sweet onions
- 1 pound of grape or cherry tomatoes
- 2 tablespoon of olive oil

Directions

- Using a larger bowl, combine the basil, salt, and vinegar.
- Introduce the onion then toss to coat.
- Let it settle for 5 minutes.
- Introduce the tomatoes, feta cheese, and oil and toss to coat.

- Serve and enjoy

Cherry tomato salad

This very recipe emerged from the need and urgency to use bumper crops of delicious cherry tomatoes commonly grown. Since then, the ingredients and directions below have been used to utilize cherry tomatoes.

Ingredients

- 1 or 2 teaspoons of minced oregano
- ¼ cup of canola oil
- ¼ cup of minced parsley
- ½ teaspoon of salt
- ½ teaspoon of sugar
- 1 quart of cherry tomatoes
- 3 tablespoons of white vinegar
- 1 teaspoon of minced basil

Directions

- In a shallow bowl, place all the tomatoes.
- In another small bowl, mix whisk oil, salt, sugar, and vinegar until evenly blended.
- Stir in the herbs.
- Pour the over tomatoes gently to toss and coat.
- Cover and refrigerate overnight.
- Serve and enjoy

Greek salad dressing

Ingredients

- ½ teaspoon of dried oregano
- ¼ teaspoon of pepper
- ½ cup of olive oil
- ½ teaspoon of salt
- ¼ cup of red wine vinegar
- 2 minced garlic cloves
- 1 teaspoon of Dijon mustard
- 2 teaspoons of lemon juice

Directions

- In a tight fitting lid jar, combine all the ingredients at once.
- Shake well until fully blended.
- Serve and enjoy.

Garden tomato salad

One can make this garden tomato recipe conveniently at any time as long as they have a garden of fresh tomatoes. The nourishing looks of a fresh tomato makes this a perfect salad for a Mediterranean Sea diet.

Ingredients

- ¼ cup of olive oil
- ½ teaspoon of salt
- 2 tablespoons of cider vinegar
- 1 minced garlic clove
- 1 teaspoon of minced chives
- 1 teaspoon of minced basil
- 1 large sweet onions cut into wedges
- 3 large tomatoes cut into wedges
- 1 large sliced cucumber

Directions

- Combine cucumber, tomatoes, and onions in a large bowl.
- In another small bowl, whisk the dressing ingredients until uniformly blended (the

remaining ingredients apart from tomatoes, cucumber, and onions)

- Drizzle over the salad then slowly toss to coat.
- Serve immediately or store under refrigeration if need be.

White bean salad

This recipe includes the preparation of white beans loaded with Mediterranean Sea diet flavors. Unlike other recipes, this one does not involve fancy dressing; as such, it is only lemon juice and extra virgin oil that is important.

Ingredients

- 1 cup chopped fresh parsley
- 4 green onions, chopped
- 1 English cucumber, diced
- 10 orzo grape or cherry tomatoes, halved
- Feta cheese, optional
- Salt and pepper
- 2 cans of rinsed and drained white beans
- 15 to 20 mint leaves, chopped
- 1 lemon, zested and juiced
- Extra virgin olive oil
- 1 teaspoon of Za'atar
- ½ teaspoon of Sumac and Aleppo .

Directions

- In a large bowl, combine the tomatoes, green onions, mint, cucumber, beans, and parsley.

- Proceed to add lemon zest.
- Season with pepper and salt.
- Add the za'atar, Aleppo pepper, and sumac.
- Finish up the recipe with lemon juice which can be drizzled with 2 or 3 tablespoon of extra virgin olive oil.
- Do a thorough toss to let combine.
- Adjust the season according to the taste.
- Introduce the feta cheese, if desired.
- Allow the salad to settle in the dressing for 30 – 31 minutes just before serving
- Serve.

3-ingredient Mediterranean salad

Ingredients

- 1 teaspoon of ground Sumac
- salt
- 2 teaspoons of freshly squeezed lemon juice
- 1 Large diced cucumber
- ½ to ¾ packed cup/ 15 to 20 g chopped fresh parsley leaves
- ½ teaspoon of black pepper
- 2 teaspoon of Early Harvest extra virgin olive oil
- 6 diced Roma tomatoes

Directions

- Put the diced tomatoes, parsley in a larger salad bowl.
- Add salt and set aside for approximately 4 minutes
- Add all remaining ingredients and toss the salad gently.
- Give the flavors some minutes to melt before serving.
- Enjoy

Traditional Greek salad

Ingredients

- 1 English cucumber partially peeled making a striped pattern
- ½ teaspoon of dried oregano
- Blocks of Greek feta cheese do not crumble the feta, leave it in large pieces
- Greek pitted Kalamata olives a handful to your liking
- 4 teaspoon of quality extra virgin olive oil
- 1 medium red onion
- kosher salt a pinch
- 4 Medium juicy tomatoes
- 1-2 teaspoon of red wine vinegar
- 1 green bell pepper cored

Instruction

- Begin by cutting the red onions into halves, then slice into crescent moon shape.
- Cut the tomatoes into wedges or even you can slice others in rounds.
- Cut the cucumber into half and slice into halves.

- The bell pepper should be sliced into rings.
- Combine all the ingredients in the above steps in a large salad dish.
- Add some pitted Kalamata olives.
- Using kosher salt, season lightly with some dried oregano.
- Pour wine vinegar and olive oil all over the salad.
- Toss gently to combine and blend. Be sure not to over mix.
- Introduce the feta block right on top and sprinkle with more of the dried oregano.
- Serve with crusty bread and enjoy.

Mediterranean watermelon salad

Watermelon a special healthy gift to the kidney can be used to make a perfect salad using only three main ingredients typically watermelon, feta cheese, cucumber. Adding fresh mint, honey vinaigrette, and basil propels this recipe to a whole new horizon.

Ingredients

- ½ peeled watermelon cut in cubes
- ½ cup of crumble feta cheese
- 15 fresh chopped mint leaves
- 15 chopped fresh basil leaves
- 1 cucumber
- 2 teaspoon of extra virgin olive oil
- 2 tablespoons of honey
- 2 teaspoons of lime juice
- Pinch of salt

Directions

- Whisk the honey together with olive oil, pinch of salt, and lime juice.
- Keep the mixture aside for a while.
- In a large bowl, serve the platter with sides.

- Combine the cucumber, fresh herbs, and watermelon together.
- Top the salad with honey vinaigrette and toss to allow massive combination.
- Top with feta cheese
- Sever and enjoy.

Mediterranean chickpea salad

Ingredients

- 1 large thinly sliced eggplant
- Salt
- oil for frying
- 1 cup cooked or canned chickpeas
- 3 tablespoons of Za'atar spice , divided
- 3 Roma tomatoes, diced
- ½ diced English cucumber, diced
- 1 small red onion, sliced in ½ moons
- 1 cup chopped parsley
- 1 cup chopped dill
- 1-2 garlic cloves, minced
- 1 large lime, juice of
- ⅓ cup Early Harvest extra virgin olive oil
- Salt and Pepper

Directions

- Place the eggplants on a tray large enough to accommodate them, then sprinkle with salt.
- Allow it to settle for 30 minutes.

- Introduce another large tray or baking sheet with paper bags topped with paper towel.
- Place it near the stove.
- Heat about 4 tablespoons of extra virgin oil after patting the eggplants dry over a medium temperature to a point of simmering.
- Fry the eggplants in batches in the oil. Ensure not to crowd the skillet.
- After the eggplants have turned golden brown on every side, remove and arrange them on a paper towel-lined tray to allowing draining and cooling.
- Assemble the eggplants on a serving dish and sprinkle with 1 tablespoon of za'atar.
- In a medium sized mixing bowl, combine the cucumbers, chickpeas, parsley, red onions, tomatoes, and the dill.
- Add the remaining za'atar and stir gently
- In a separate small bowl, whisk the dressing together.
- Drizzle 2 tablespoons of the salad dressing over the already fried eggplants.

- The remaining dressing should be poured over the chickpeas salad mix.
- Add the chickpea salad to the eggplant in a serving dish.
- Enjoy.

Chicken sharwarma salad bowls

Ingredients

- ¾ tablespoon of garlic powder
- Salt
- ¾ tablespoon of paprika
- ¾ tablespoon of ground coriander
- 8 boneless, skinless chicken thighs
- ¾ tablespoon of ground cumin
- ½ teaspoon of ground cloves
- ½ teaspoon of cayenne pepper
- ¾ tablespoon of turmeric powder
- ⅓ cup extra virgin olive oil
- 1 large onion, thinly sliced
- 1 large lemon, juice of
- 1 garlic clove minced
- 8 oz. baby arugula
- 2 to 3 Roma tomatoes, diced
- Sumac approximately ½ teaspoon
- Juice of 1 lemon
- Extra Virgin Olive Oil
- ¼ red onion, thinly sliced

- 1 English cucumber, diced
- Salt and pepper

Directions

- In a small bowl, mix majority of the ingredients typically the coriander, turmeric, cumin, garlic power, paprika, and cloves.
- Keep the sharwarma spice for later
- Pat the chicken thighs dry and season with salt on both sides.
- Then thinly slice into small bite-sized pieces.
- Put the chicken in a large bowl, then add the shawarma spices, then toss to coat.
- Introduce the onions, olive oil, and lemon juice.
- Toss everything together to combine, then set aside as you prepare the salad
- Cover totally for refrigeration for up to 3 hours. If there is time for you to wait, refrigerate overnight.
- Prepare the salad in a mixing bowl by combining the tomatoes, cucumbers, arugula, and onions over a medium temperature.

- In a separate small bowl combine the olive oil, garlic, pepper, salt, sumac, and lemon juice to make the dressing, blend thoroughly well.
- Pour the dressing over the salad and toss to let combine.
- Heat another extra virgin olive oil in a large skillet over medium temperature until when it simmers without smoke.
- Add the chicken and let cook for 5 – 6 minutes.
- Toss and continue to cook for another 5 – 6 minute until when the chicken is ready.
- Divide the salad into serving dishes, then add the ready cooked chicken sharwarma.
- Serve and enjoy with pit wedges if desired.

Mediterranean couscous salad

This salad recipe is yet loaded with flavorful and highly nutritious from sources such as fresh herbs, chickpeas, zippy lemon dill vinaigrette. Other than that, the dish is famous for its versatility for lunch, supper and or breakfast. Interestingly, it can be made ahead of time before hunger hunts you down.

Ingredients

- 15-20 fresh basil leaves, roughly chopped or torn
- Water
- 1 tsp dill weed
- 15 ounces can chickpeas
- 2 cups Pearl Couscous
- salt and pepper
- Private Reserve extra virgin olive oil
- 1 large lemon, juice of
- 14 ounces can artichoke hearts
- ⅓ cup extra virgin olive oil
- ½ English cucumber, chopped
- 2 cups grape tomatoes, halved

- ½ cup pitted Kalamata olive
- ⅓ cup finely chopped red onions
- 1 to 2 garlic cloves, minced
- 3 ounces of fresh baby mozzarella optional

Directions

- Place all the vinaigrette ingredients in a bowl to make the lemon-dill vinaigrette.
- Whisk together to combine keep aside for a short while.
- In a medium-sized pot, heat two tablespoons of olive oil .
- Briefly, Sauté the couscous in the olive oil to turn golden brown.
- Add boiling water about 3 cups or as instructed to cook the couscous.
- Drain excess water in a colander when ready and also keep aside in a bowl allow to cool.
- Combine all the remaining ingredients except the basil and mozzarella in a large mixing bowl.
- Add the couscous and the basil and mix together gently

- It is time to give the lemon-dill vinaigrette a quick whisk, also add to the couscous salad.
- Mix again to combine.
- Test and adjust the salt accordingly.
- Lastly, mix in the mozzarella cheese and garnish with more fresh basil.
- Serve and enjoy.

Mediterranean cauliflower salad

Ingredients

- Extra virgin olive oil
- 1 whole bunch of parsley, stems partially removed
- Kosher salt and pepper
- 1 English cucumber chopped
- ½ red onion, chopped
- 1 head raw cauliflower, cut into florets
- 1 to 2 garlic cloves, minced
- 3 – 4 Roma tomatoes, chopped
- Juice of 2 lemons

Directions

- In a bowl of a food processor fitted with a blade, put the cauliflower florets.
- Pulse briefly until the cauliflower turns rice-like in texture.
- Move chopped cauliflower into a larger bowl.
- Add the parsley, cucumbers, tomatoes, and onions let toss to combine.
- Add minced garlic and season with salt and pepper.

- Add fresh lemon juice and drizzle with extra virgin olive oil.
- Toss once again to combine.
- Keep the cauliflower salad aside for some minutes let soften and absorb dressing.
- Serve and enjoy.

Watermelon cups

This recipe is largely and appetizer pretty and sweet to enjoy. In addition, watermelon is a gift to the kidney which boosts its functionality. The watermelon cut into cubes hold with a refreshing topping that shows red onions, fresh herbs and cucumber brings out a person's appetite to eat them.

Ingredients

- 15 – 17 watermelon cubes without seeds
- 5 teaspoons of red onions finely chopped
- 2 teaspoons of mint freshly minced
- 1/3 cups of chopped cucumber
- 2 teaspoons of fresh cilantro minced
- ½ teaspoon of lime juice

Directions

- In a watermelon baller, measure spoon, scoop the watermelon blossoms form the center of the cubes.
- Do not totally remove the center of the watermelon, leave about 1/4 in

- Mix all the remaining ingredients in a separate small bowl
- Spoon it into watermelon cubes
- Serve and enjoy your watermelon cups for a healthy kidney

Simple green juice

15 minutes is all it takes to make this handful 6 ingredients healthy juice with its refreshing tast

Ingredients

- 5 celery stalks, ends trimmed
- Handful fresh parsley, 1 ounce
- 1 Inch piece of fresh peeled ginger
- 1 bunch kale, 5 ounces
- ½ large English cucumber
- 1 Granny smith apple

Directions

- Prep all the vegetables after washing.
- Add all the ingredients into a juicer and blend at once.
- Pour the green juice to glasses and serve immediately.
- Enjoy.

Mixed beery smoothie

If you do not like chopping of ingredient, then this is a perfect Mediterranean smoothie you can go for. It gets ready in only 5 minutes. All you need is to blend all the ingredients at once.

Ingredients

- ⅛ cup honey
- ⅓ cup Greek yogurt
- 2 ripe bananas
- 2 cups frozen mixed berry
- 1 cup milk

Directions

- In a blender, combine bananas together with the, frozen berry mix, milk, Greek yogurt, and honey.
- Blend until finely smooth.
- Serve and enjoy.

Apple pear ginger smoothie

This is a dairy free recipe with variety of fruits and ginger as a flavor. It is rich with antioxidants and vitamins from the 5 ingredients.

Ingredients

- 1½ cup of apple juice
- ½ cup rolled oats
- 1 thumb-size ginger, finely grated
- 3 pears cored and diced
- 3 apples preferably red, peeled and diced

Directions

- Process the oats until they are powdery in a food processor.
- Add the remaining ingredients, process until smooth
- Serve and enjoy immediately.

Detox green juice

Among the Mediterranean Sea diet recipes, detox green juice is a perfect immunity booster and a body cleanser. It takes 10 minutes to prepare.

Ingredients

- ½ small lemon, juice only
- 7 ounces of fresh kale
- ½ English of cucumber
- 3 large green apples
- 1 cup fresh spinach

Directions

- Cut the apples into quarters, kale, and cucumber pieces
- Using a juicer, juice everything else apart from the lemon.
- Taste and adjust accordingly with lemon.
- Serve and enjoy.

Mango kale smoothie

A combination of mango and kale (herb) makes a wonderful healthy smoothie packed with vitamins and antioxidants.

Ingredients

- 2 tablespoons of honey
- 1 medium banana, cut into chunks
- ½ cup of Greek yogurt
- 1 cup of frozen mango pieces
- 2 cups of chopped kale leaves
- 1 cup of milk

Directions

- Combine every ingredient into a blender.
- Blend until it becomes smooth.
- Transfer into a glass.
- Serve and enjoy.

Matcha iced tea

Matcha iced tea is a perfect Mediterranean Sea diet for a refreshing drink with mint and a ton of flavors.

Ingredients

- 1 lime
- 1 cup of crushed ice
- 2 teaspoon of matcha powder
- 2 cups of cold water
- 5 tablespoon of maple syrup
- 1/4 cup of hot water
- 3 sprigs of fresh mint

Directions

- Combine and mix matcha powder in water in a small dish, mix.
- Place in crushed ice, cold water together with fresh mint in a blender.
- Add in the matcha tea blend briefly for 1 minute.
- Drain.
- Add juice and maple syrup after half of the time has run up.

- Garnish with mint leaves and lime.
- Serve and enjoy.

Mediterranean green salad

This recipe is a perfect outdoor or entertainment recipe or grill parties. It only takes 10 minutes.

Ingredients

- 1 butter lettuce
- 2 tablespoons of honey
- A few fresh mint leaves
- 1 tablespoon of lemon juice
- 2 spring onions
- 2 cups of fresh sweet peas
- 2 green peppers
- 1½ cup cherry tomatoes
- 5 tablespoons of extra virgin olive oil
- 1 cup of mange tout

Directions

- Cut lettuce into thin strips
- Shell the peas.
- Slice the spring onions.
- Cut green peppers into thin strips.
- Half the tomatoes.

- Combine all the ingredients i.e. olive oil, chopped mint leaves. lemon juice, and honey.
- Pour over the salad.
- Serve and enjoy.

Strawberry salad with poppy seeds dressing

This recipe is a typical side dish for a BBQ combined with strawberries, spring onions and lettuce. It gets ready in only 10 minutes.

Ingredients

- 1 tablespoon of balsamic reduction
- 4 tablespoons of extra virgin olive oil
- 2 cups of fresh strawberries
- 2 tablespoons of poppy seeds
- 1 head of butter lettuce
- 2 spring onions

Directions

- Clean and chop the ingredients and place them in a serving dish.
- Mix them together with hands.
- Combine extra virgin olive oil, poppy seeds, and balsamic reduction. Mix well in a jar.
- Pour the mixture over the salad.
- Serve and enjoy immediately.

Mega crunchy romaine salad with quinoa

Ingredients

- ½ cup of raw sunflower seeds
- ½ teaspoon of grain sea salt
- 1 small head of romaine
- 1 cup of shredded carrots
- ¼ teaspoon of chili powder
- 2 teaspoons of honey
- 1 cup of chopped cabbage
- ½ cup of chopped radishes
- 2 medium cloves garlic
- ½ cup of dried cranberries
- ⅓ cup of olive oil
- ⅔ cup of uncooked quinoa
- 3 tablespoons of lime juice
- 2 tablespoons of rice vinegar
- 1 ⅓ cups of water
- ¼ cup of fresh cilantro

Directions

- Bring the mixture of quinoa and water to a boil over medium-high heat.

- Lower the heat, let simmer. Cook until the quinoa has absorbed all of the water.
- Remove, let the quinoa steam for 5 minutes.
- Combine the sunflower seeds and olive oil in a medium skillet.
- Cook, stirring frequently over medium heat, until the seeds are fragrant.
- Remove, set aside to cool.
- In a large serving bowl, combine the carrots, cabbage, radishes, prepared romaine, and cranberries.
- Add quinoa and sunflower seed to the bowl as well.
- Combine the olive oil, rice vinegar, cilantro, honey, garlic, sea salt, and chili powder, blend in a blender.
- Serve and enjoy.

Thai mango salad with peanut dressing

Ingredients

- 1 head of butter leaf lettuce
- 1 tablespoon of apple cider vinegar
- 1 teaspoon of sesame oil
- 1 red bell pepper
- 3 ripe champagne mangos, diced
- 2 cloves garlic
- ½ cup of sliced green onion
- ⅓ cup of chopped roasted peanuts
- ¼ cup of chopped fresh cilantro
- 1 tablespoon of honey
- Pinch of red pepper flakes
- 1 medium jalapeño
- ¼ cup of creamy peanut butter
- ¼ cup of lime juice
- 1 tablespoon of tamari

Directions

- Combine butter leaf lettuce, red bell pepper, mango, onion, roasted peanut, cilantro, and jalapeno in a large serving bowl.

- Combine peanut butter, lime juice, tamari, apple cider vinegar, honey, sesame, garlic, and pepper flakes in a bowl, and whisk to combine.
- Drizzle the dressing over the salad, toss to combine.
- Serve and enjoy.

Crispy apple and kohlrabi salad

Ingredients

- 2 tablespoons of lemon juice
- 1 large Honey crisp apple
- ¼ cup of fresh tarragon leaves
- Flaky sea salt
- 2 small kohlrabies
- 3 tablespoons of toasted sunflower seeds
- Lemon zest, to taste
- 2 tablespoons olive oil

Directions

- In a large serving bowl, combine the kohlrabi together with the apple matchsticks.
- Add the cheese with sunflower seeds.
- Drizzle in bit of olive oil and some lemon juice
- Sprinkle lightly with salt and black pepper.
- Toss the salad with your hands.
- Serve and enjoy.

Sundried tomato, spinach, and quinoa salad

Ingredients

- ½ teaspoon of salt
- 1 cup of quinoa
- ⅓ cup of sun-dried tomatoes
- 1 teaspoon of Dijon mustard
- Pinch of red pepper flakes
- 2 cups of roughly chopped fresh spinach
- ⅓ cup of sliced almonds
- Freshly ground black pepper
- 2 cloves garlic
- ¼ teaspoon of olive oil
- Salt, to taste
- 2 tablespoons of olive oil
- 2 tablespoons of lemon juice

Directions

- Combine quinoa and 2 cups water in a medium saucepan.
- Bring the mixture to a boil over medium-high heat.

- Simmer over low heat, until the quinoa has absorbed all of the water.
- Remove, let the quinoa rest for 5 minutes.
- Whisk together the olive oil with lemon juice, garlic, mustard, salt and red pepper flakes.
- Season with freshly ground black pepper.
- Warm bit of olive oil over medium heat until shimmering.
- Add the almonds and a dash of salt, let cook, stirring frequently until golden.
- Let the almonds cool.
- Transfer the quinoa to the serving bowl.
- Drizzle all of the dressing on top, toss to combine.
- Add the chopped sun-dried tomatoes and spinach.
- Serve and enjoy.

Berry spinach salad with spicy maple sunflower seeds

Ingredients

- ½ teaspoon of Dijon mustard
- 1 tablespoon of balsamic vinegar
- ⅓ cup of sunflower seeds
- 1 ½ teaspoons of maple syrup
- ⅓ cup of crumbled goat cheese
- Pinch salt
- Salt and pepper
- Dash cayenne
- 5 ounces of baby spinach
- 1 ½ cups of total raspberries
- ½ teaspoon of maple syrup
- 3 tablespoons of olive oil

Directions

- Warm a small non-stick skillet over medium heat, add the sunflower seeds.
- When the seeds warm up, pour in the maple syrup, a pinch of salt and a tiny dash of cayenne pepper, toast while stirring constantly

until most of the maple syrup has evaporated in 5 minutes.

- Transfer the seeds to a plate.
- In a serving bowl, combine the spinach with the berries, crumbled goat cheese, and sunflower seeds.
- Whisk olive oil, balsamic vinegar, Dijon mustard, maple syrup, salt and pepper until emulsified.
- Serve and enjoy.

Summertime pasta salad with tomatoes, corn, and jalapeno pesto

Ingredients

- ½ teaspoon of salt
- ½ cup of olive oil
- 1 can of black beans
- 1-pint of cherry tomatoes
- 1 ear of fresh corn, shucked
- Freshly ground black pepper
- ½ pound of whole grain bow-tie pasta
- ¾ cup crumbled feta
- 1 cup of fresh parsley
- 1 cup of cilantro
- ½ cup of pepitas
- 2 medium jalapeños
- 1 medium lemon, juiced
- 1 medium garlic clove

Directions

- Bring a large pot of salted water to boil.
- Cook the pasta according to package directions.

- Drain, reserve some cooking water.
- Toast the pepitas in a small skillet over medium heat, stirring frequently, until lightly golden on the edges.
- Combine the herbs, jalapeño, lemon, garlic, and salt in a food processor.
- Pour in the pepitas.
- Pulse while drizzling in the olive oil until the mixture is well blended.
- Pour enough pesto into the pasta to lightly coat it once tossed.
- Add a small splash of pasta cooking water and toss well.
- Transfer the pasta to a large serving bowl.
- Add the drained black beans, sliced cherry tomatoes, fresh corn and feta.
- Serve and enjoy.

Tropical mango spring rolls with avocado cilantro dipping sauce

Ingredients

- ½ cup of lightly packed fresh cilantro
- 2 ripe mangos
- ⅓ cup of water
- ½ teaspoon of salt
- 1 large red bell pepper
- 2 jalapeños
- 4 green onions
- 7 round of rice papers
- 3 cups of arugula
- 2 ripe avocados, diced
- ⅓ cup of lime juice

Directions

- Fill a shallow pan with warm water. Fold a lint-free tea towel in half and place it next to the dish.
- Place one rice paper in the water and let it rest for 20 seconds. Carefully lay it flat on the towel.

- Cover the lower third of the paper with chopped arugula.
- Top with 4 slices of mango down the length of the greens.
- Then, followed by several slices of bell pepper and jalapeño, sprinkle of green onions.
- Fold over one long side to enclose the filling, then fold over the short sides, roll it up. Repeat with remaining ingredients.
- Combine the avocado, lime juice, water, cilantro, and salt in a small food processor.
- Purée until smooth and transfer to a small serving bowl.
- Serve and enjoy.

Greek kale salad with creamy tahini dressing

This Mediterranean Sea diet recipe features very bold Mediterranean flavors making it a healthier and tastier recipe.

Ingredients

- Freshly ground black pepper
- ½ cup of thinly sliced Kalamata olives
- ⅓ cup of finely grated Parmesan
- ⅓ cup of sunflower seeds
- ¼ teaspoon of extra-virgin olive oil
- 3 tablespoons of lemon juice
- 1 tablespoon of extra-virgin olive oil
- 1 medium clove garlic, pressed
- Fine sea salt
- ¼ cup of tahini
- ½ teaspoon of Dijon mustard
- ⅓ cup of oil-packed sun-dried tomatoes, rinsed and drained
- ¼ teaspoon of fine sea salt
- 1 can of chickpeas, rinsed and drained

- 2 tablespoons of water
- 1 medium bunch of curly green kale

Directions

- Put chopped kale in a large serving bowl.
- Sprinkle it lightly with salt and massage with your hands.
- Add the chickpeas together with the olives and pepper rings, sun-dried tomatoes, and Parmesan keep aside.
- Combine the sunflower seeds with the olive oil and a few dashes of salt in a small skillet over medium heat.
- Let cook for 5 minutes, stirring frequently, until the seeds are turning lightly golden at the edges.
- Pour the toasted seeds into the salad bowl.
- In a small bowl, combine the tahini together with the olive oil, lemon juice, garlic, mustard, and salt.
- Whisk to blend completely.
- Add the water and whisk until blended.
- Season with freshly black pepper.

- Pour the dressing into the salad toss to equally coat the salad.
- Serve and enjoy immediately.
- Any leftovers can be refrigerated.

Vegetarian stuffed cabbage rolls

This cabbage is rolled with vegetarian rice filling loaded with various herbs and vegetables especially onions, tomatoes and spices to give the recipe a delicious taste.

Ingredients

- ¼ cup of extra virgin olive oil
- ½ cup of shredded yellow onion
- 2 Roma tomato sliced
- 1 tomato, chopped or diced
- 1 medium green cabbage
- 1 medium yellow onion sliced
- ½ cup of chopped fresh parsley
- ½ cup of chopped fresh dill
- 1 teaspoon of ground cumin
- Water
- ½ teaspoon of cayenne pepper
- ½ teaspoon of ground allspice
- Salt and pepper
- 1 15-oz. can of tomato sauce, divided
- 1 cup of long-grain rice

Directions

- Remove and discard the first couple leaves of cabbage and clean in cold water.
- Cut off the bottom then place the whole head of cabbage in boiling water, let boil 2 minutes.
- Peel off the softened leaves, continue with the same process, peeling off the blanched layers of cabbage leaves as they soften.
- Cut each cabbage leaf into halves, removing any thick veins.
- In a large mixing bowl, combine the rice together with the shredded onions, herbs, spices, salt and pepper, chopped tomato, tomato sauce and water. Mix together.
- Lightly oil a large heavy cooking pot.
- Line the bottom with the sliced onions and sliced tomatoes.
- Take a piece of cabbage and place on a flat surface, coarse side up.
- Add 1 teaspoon of rice stuffing mixture at the end of the leaf closest to you.

- Roll up the leaf to completely enclose the stuffing.
- Repeat with all the remaining cabbage.
- Layer the cabbage rolls, in the prepared pot.
- Top with the remaining tomato sauce, and water.
- Add a pinch of ground cumin.
- Top the cabbage rolls with a small plate.
- For 7 minutes, cook on high heat until the liquid reduces to half.
- Lower the leaving the small plate in, and cover the pot with its own lid.
- Continue to cook for 30 minutes, then remove the plate leave the lid to cover it.
- Cook for more 15 minutes to absorb all the liquid.
- Le the cabbage rolls rest for some time.
- Serve and enjoy.

Herbed couscous recipe with roasted cauliflower

Herbs are another heart of the Mediterranean Sea diet. As a result, this herbed couscous recipe with roasted cauliflower blends herbs with other flavors to give it a required taste to satisfy your taste buds.

Ingredients

For roasted cauliflower

- ½ teaspoon of black pepper
- Greek extra virgin olive oil
- 1 ½ teaspoon of sweet Spanish paprika
- ¾ teaspoon of cumin
- ¾ teaspoon of salt, more for later
- 1 head cauliflower, divided into small florets
- 1 ½ teaspoon of za'atar , more for later
- ½ teaspoon of cayenne pepper, optional

For Couscous

- 8 oz. uncooked pearl
- 1 3-Ingredient Mediterranean Salad
- 1 cup packed chopped fresh parsley
- Feta cheese

- 2 green onions, trimmed, both white and greens chopped
- Greek extra virgin olive oil
- 1 tahini sauce recipe
- 2 teaspoons of fresh lemon juice

Directions

- Preheat oven to 475°F.
- In a small bowl, spices, salt, and pepper.
- Make sure to set aside 1 tablespoon of the spice mixture for later.
- Place the cauliflower on a large sheet pan.
- Drizzle with extra virgin olive oil.
- Sprinkle the spice mixture on top of the cauliflower. Toss by hand to co\t well.
- Spread on the sheet pan in one layer.
- Cover the sheet pan with foil.
- Place on the bottom rack of the heated oven.
- Let bake for 10 minutes.
- Remove from oven and uncover.
- Return to heated oven, let bake for more 15 minutes.

- Remove again from oven, turn cauliflower over on the other side.
- Return to oven for another 12 minutes.
- Prepare the simple Mediterranean salad normally. Prepare he tahini sauce normally.
- In a saucepan, heat 1 tablespoon of extra virgin olive oil over medium heat.
- Add couscous and the remaining 1 tablespoon of spice mixture.
- Sauté, tossing regularly, until couscous is toasted into a light brown color.
- Add boiling water. Turn heat to low, cover and simmer for 12 minutes or until liquid is absorbed and couscous is fully cooked.
- Remove cooked couscous from heat source.
- Add chopped green onions, parsley, and lemon juice. Mix.
- Divide herbed couscous and roasted cauliflower among 4 dinner bowls.
- Add 3-ingredient Mediterranean salad to each.
- Sprinkle with feta cheese and a pinch of Za'atar.

- Drizzle a little tahini over the cauliflower.
- Serve and enjoy.

Fresh fava bean salad and fava spread

The flavor of this fresh fava bean is amazing with olive, lemon juice which can be turned to a delicious fava spread.

Ingredients

- 1 cup of bread cubes
- ½ cup of Kalamata olives, sliced
- ½ cup of chopped parsley
- 1 tablespoon of lemon juice, or to taste
- 2 tablespoons of olive oil
- 2 pounds of whole fresh fava beans in their pods
- 1 teaspoon of dried oregano
- Freshly ground black pepper to taste
- 3 tablespoons of olive oil

Directions

- Start by preheat your oven ready to 350°F.
- Then, brush the bread cubes with the olive oil.
- Let bake for about 15 minutes or until the color turns golden.
- Allow them to cool for 10 minutes.

- Snap the fava pods in the meantime, and collect the fava beans in a bowl.
- Set a medium pot filled with water over high heat.
- Bring to a boil.
- Then, add the fava beans let boil for 1 minute.
- Drain any excess water with a colander, make sure to rinse with cold water until fava beans are no longer warm.
- Now, cut the top of the membrane of each bean with a paring knife.
- Squeeze it all with your fingers.
- Make sure the bean can easily slide out quickly and swiftly.
- Repeat this with all of the remaining beans.
- Mix the shelled fava beans together with the croutons and the rest of the ingredients in a bowl.
- After mixing, serve in your eating dish and enjoy immediately or when still warm.

Mega crunchy romaine salad with quinoa

Ingredient

For the Salad

- 1 ⅓ cups of water
- ½ teaspoon of olive oil
- ½ cup of chopped radishes
- ⅔ cup of uncooked quinoa, rinsed
- 1 small head of romaine
- ½ cup of raw sunflower seeds
- 1 cup of shredded carrots
- 1 cup of chopped cabbage
- ½ cup of dried cranberries

For the Zippy cilantro dressing

- ¼ cup of lightly packed fresh cilantro
- 2 teaspoons of honey or maple syrup
- ¼ teaspoon of chipotle chili powder
- 2 medium cloves garlic, roughly chopped
- ⅓ cup of olive oil
- ½ teaspoon of fine-grain sea salt
- 2 tablespoons of rice vinegar
- 3 tablespoons of lime juice

Directions

- Combine the quinoa together with the water in a medium saucepan.
- Bring to a boil over medium-high heat.
- Lower the heat a bit to maintain a gentle simmer.
- Let cook until the quinoa has absorbed all of the liquid in 15 minutes.
- Reduce the heat further as time goes on to maintain a gentle simmer.
- Remove the pot from heat.
- Then, cover let the steam for 5 minutes, set aside for later.
- Combine the sunflower seeds and olive oil in a medium skillet.
- Let cook over medium heat, keep stirring frequently till the seeds start to turn lightly golden on the edges.
- Remove from heat and set aside to cool.
- In another large bowl, combine the prepared romaine, carrots, cabbage, radishes and cranberries.

- Add them to the bowl as well when the quinoa and the sunflower is ready.
- In a blender, combine olive oil, lime juice, rice vinegar, cilantro, maple syrup, garlic, sea salt, and chipotle chili powder.
- Blend well, pausing to scrape down the sides.
- Taste and adjust accordingly.
- Drizzle in enough dressing to lightly coat the salad once tossed.
- Serve and enjoy.

Southwestern kale power salad with sweet potato, quinoa, and avocado sauce

Ingredients

For the Quinoa and kale

- ½ teaspoon of salt
- 1 medium lime, juiced
- 1 cup of quinoa
- 2 tablespoons of olive oil
- 1 bunch of kale, ribs removed and chopped

For the Sweet potatoes

- 2 medium sweet potatoes
- 1 ½ teaspoons of salt
- 2 tablespoons of olive oil
- 1 teaspoon of smoked paprika
- 2 teaspoons of ground cumin

For the Avocado sauce

- ⅓ cup of crumbled feta, omit for vegan
- ¼ cup of pepitas
- Salt
- 2 avocados, sliced into long strips
- 2 limes, juiced

- 1 handful cilantro leaves
- ½ teaspoon of ground coriander
- 2 tablespoons olive oil
- 1 can of black beans, rinsed and drained
- 1 medium jalapeño, deseeded, membranes removed

Directions

- Clean the quinoa and in a medium-sized pot, combine the rinsed quinoa and 2 cups water.
- Bring the mixture to a gentle boil covered.
- Lower the heat to a simmer let cook for 15 minutes.
- Remove the quinoa from heat source and let rest covered for 5 minutes.
- Uncover the pot, drain off any excess water and fluff the quinoa with a fork.
- Set it aside to cool.
- In another large skillet, warm the olive oil over medium heat.
- Add the chopped sweet potatoes and toss to coat.

- Add the cumin together with the smoked paprika and salt. Stir to combine.
- Add a scant ¼ cup of water and cover the pan once the pan is sizzling.
- Lower the heat to avoid burning the contents.
- Let cook as you keep stirring occasionally, until the sweet potato is tender.
- Raise the heat when uncovered to medium let cook until the excess moisture has evaporated in 7 minutes and the sweet potatoes are caramelizing on the edges. Let cool.
- Transfer the kale to a large mixing bowl.
- Sprinkle the chopped kale with salt and massage with your hands
- Whisk together 2 tablespoons olive oil, the juice of 1 lime and ½ teaspoon salt.
- Drizzle over the kale and toss to coat.
- Combine the avocados, lime juice, olive oil, jalapeno, cilantro leaves, coriander, and salt in a blender.
- Blend well then season with salt.

- In a small skillet over medium-low heat, toast the pepitas, stirring frequently, until they are turning lightly golden on the edges in 5 minutes.
- Once the quinoa has cooled down a bit, pour it into the bowl of kale and toss to combine.
- Divide the kale and quinoa mixture into four large salad bowls.
- Top with sweet potatoes, black beans, a big dollop of avocado sauce, and a sprinkle of feta and pepitas.
- Serve and enjoy.

Sundried tomato Caesar salad

Ingredients

For the parmesan crusted croutons

- ½ cup of grated Parmesan
- 3 tablespoons of olive oil
- 2 cups of ¾-inch cubes of rustic bread
- ¼ teaspoon of salt

For the sundried tomato dressing

- Pinch sea salt
- ½ cup of grated Parmesan
- 2 tablespoons of freshly squeezed lemon juice
- Freshly ground black pepper
- ¼ cup of roughly chopped sun-dried tomatoes
- ½ cup of extra-virgin olive oil
- 2 tablespoons of water
- 1 garlic clove, roughly chopped

For the Caesar salad

- Sprinkle of additional chopped sun-dried tomatoes
- Sprinkle of additional Parmesan
- 2 small heads of romaine

Directions

- Begin by soaking the sundried tomatoes boiling water until they're pliable, then pat them dry.
- Next, preheat your oven to 400°F with a rack in the top of the oven.
- Line a baking sheet with parchment paper.
- Mix the olive oil together with the Parmesan and salt in a large mixing bowl until a paste is formed.
- Add the cubed bread and mix well with a spatula, until all the bread is coated.
- Turn the bread onto the prepared baking sheet and arrange in a single layer.
- Let bake for 10 minutes, then stir and put the croutons back into the oven until they are golden brown in more 5 minutes.
- Combine the sun-dried tomatoes together with the Parmesan, lemon juice, water, garlic and a pinch of salt in a food processor.
- Blend briefly for 1 minute, stopping to scrape down the sides if needed.

- While running the machine, drizzle in the olive oil and blend for 10 more seconds.
- Taste and adjust accordingly. Set aside.
- Drizzle the dressing over your halved romaine.
- Finish with croutons and a sprinkle of Parmesan and sun-dried tomatoes.
- Serve and enjoy immediately.

Chorizo tomato and charred corn salad

Ingredients

- Cayenne pepper
- 3 Spanish Chorizo sausage links, casings removed
- 1 teaspoon of sumac
- 1 loaf of rustic country
- Salt and pepper
- 2 garlic cloves, sliced
- Dried mint or parsley flakes
- 1 corn on the cob
- olive oil
- 3 tablespoon of aged white wine vinegar
- 2 large tomatoes
- 1 shallot, sliced
- 1 cup of baby spinach

Directions

- Begin by heating a cast iron grill.
- Add the corn to the hot skillet and grill, rotating on all sides, until it is nicely charred.
- Remove from the skillet and let cool.
- Place a small bowl, in a large salad bowl.

- After the corn has cooled enough to handle, place it on top of the small bowl and, with a sharp knife, begin to slice through the kernels.
- Set the large bowl with the corn kernels aside for later.
- Turn the heat to medium-high.
- Add 2 tablespoon of olive oil to the cast iron skillet.
- In the heated oil, brown the Chorizo sausage as you toss frequently, until fully cooked.
- Add the garlic slices and toss briefly.
- Remove the skillet from the heat.
- Stir in the white wine vinegar. Set aside.
- Add the tomato wedges together with the baby spinach, shallots and spices.
- Drizzle with olive oil toss.
- Add the cooked Chorizo with the garlic and vinegar, toss.
- Taste and adjust the seasoning accordingly.
- Transfer to serving bowls and garnish with dried mint flakes.
- Serve and enjoy with rustic bread.

Tangy lentil salad with dill and pepperoncini

Ingredients

- ½ cup of chopped pickled pepperoncini pepper
- 1 ½ cups of black beluga lentils
- ½ cup of tiny cubes of Havarti
- 2 tablespoons of tahini
- 1 bay leaf
- Freshly ground black pepper
- ¼ cup of fresh dill leaves, tough stems removed
- ⅓ cup of extra-virgin olive oil
- 2 cups of grated carrots
- ½ teaspoon of red pepper flakes
- ¼ cup of fresh dill leaves, tough stems removed
- ½ cup of chopped celery
- ½ cup of thinly sliced green onion
- ¼ cup of lemon juice
- 1 clove garlic, roughly chopped

- ¾ cup of fresh flat-leaf parsley
- Fine sea salt

Directions

- Fill a large saucepan with water and boil over high heat.
- When the water is boiling, add the rinsed lentils.
- Add the bay leaf and salt.
- Set the timer for 16 minutes.
- Reduce the heat to prevent overflow and maintain lively simmer.
- Combine the olive oil together with the dill, lemon juice, garlic, tahini, salt, red pepper flakes and several twists of black pepper.
- Blend until smooth, set aside for later.
- When the time is up, scoop out a few lentils and test for doneness.
- Strain off all the excess water in the lentil.
- Pour the lentils into a medium serving bowl as you discard the bay leaf.
- Pour in all of the dressing, stir to combine.

- Add the grated carrots together with the parsley, celery, green onion, the remaining dill, and pepperoncini peppers.
- When the lentils are warm, add the optional cheese.
- Stir the mixture to combine.
- Season to taste accordingly.
- Let it sit for 20 minutes.
- Serve and enjoy.
- Keep the left over refrigerated.

Mustard potato salad, Mediterranean style

The recipe contains fresh dill, parsley, red onions as well as caper for a great Mediterranean diet. The Dijon mustard dressing is used to dress the potatoes when still hot for a perfect flavor absorption.

Ingredients

- Water
- ¼ cup of chopped red onions
- ½ teaspoon of ground sumac
- Teaspoon of salt
- ¼ teaspoon of ground coriander
- ¼ cup of fresh chopped parsley
- 2 tablespoons of capers
- ⅓ cup of extra virgin olive oil
- 2 tablespoons of white wine vinegar
- 1 ½ lb. small potatoes
- ¼ cup of chopped dill
- 2 teaspoon of Dijon mustard
- ½ teaspoon of black pepper

Directions

- Wash slice potatoes thinly.
- Place potatoes in a pot and add water to cover, boil.
- Add salt.
- Lower the let simmer for 6 minutes or so until tender.
- Add vinaigrette ingredients to a small bowl and whisk until combined.
- Remove from heat and drain well.
- Place them in a large mixing bowl and immediately dress them with the Dijon mustard dressing, toss to coat.
- Add onions, fresh herbs, and capers. Toss to combine.
- Transfer the potatoes to a serving platter let settle for 1 hour.
- Serve and enjoy.

Caponata recipe

The caponata recipe is largely are tasty salad made relish of eggplants and onions, celery as well as tomatoes to bring out the real taste of a Mediterranean Sea diet salad.

Ingredients

- Extra virgin olive oil
- 1 yellow onion chopped
- 1 red bell pepper cored and chopped
- ¼ cup of dry white wine
- 2 tablespoons of chopped fresh mint
- ¼ cup of red wine vinegar
- Kosher salt
- 2 small celery stalks thinly sliced
- Black pepper
- 2 tablespoons of capers
- ¼ cup of pitted green olives roughly chopped
- ¼ cup of raisins
- 1 large eggplant
- 2 teaspoons of honey more to your liking
- 1 bay leaf
- 1 cup of crushed tomatoes

- ¼ teaspoon of crushed red pepper flakes
- 2 tablespoons of chopped fresh parsley

Directions

- Heat your oven to 400°F.
- Season the eggplant cubes with salt 30 minutes to sweat out the bitterness.
- Place the seasoned eggplant cubes on a sheet pan, add a drizzle of extra virgin olive oil, toss.
- Roast the eggplant in the heated oven for 25 – 30 minutes.
- Heat 2 tablespoons of extra virgin olive oil in a large skillet.
- Add the onions together with the bell pepper, and celery.
- Season with a pinch of kosher salt and black pepper.
- Let cook for 7 minutes, tossing regularly.
- Add the tomatoes together with the capers, olives, honey, raisins, bay leaf and crushed pepper flakes.
- Pour in the vinegar and white wine. Stir to combine.

- Simmer over low heat for 10 minutes.
- Stir in the roasted eggplant and continue to cook for 3 minutes in the sauce.
- Finish with fresh parsley and mint.
- Serve and enjoy.

Blanched asparagus recipe with Mediterranean salsa

This asparagus recipe is fully parked with Mediterranean salsa with tomatoes, fresh herbs and shallots. It can be served as an appetizer for a vegan dish.

Ingredients

- Zest of 1 lemon
- 1 garlic clove finely chopped
- ¼ cup of chopped fresh mint leaves
- 1 shallot finely chopped
- 12 oz. of cherry tomatoes chopped or halved
- ½ teaspoon of sumac
- 3 teaspoons of fresh lemon juice
- Greek extra virgin olive oil more for later
- ½ cup of chopped fresh parsley leaves
- 1 ½ lb. of Asparagus tough ends trimmed
- Water
- Salt and pepper

Directions

- In a mixing bowl, add the tomatoes together with the shallots, garlic and herbs.

- Season with salt, pepper, and sumac.
- Add lemon juice and a drizzle of extra virgin olive oil. Mix and keep for later.
- In a cooking pot, boil 8 cups of water, seasoned with 2 tablespoons of kosher salt.
- Add the prepared asparagus. Boil for 4 minutes until tender.
- Drain any excess water and immediately transfer to a bowl of ice water briefly to stop the cooking process.
- Drain and let cool.
- Arrange the asparagus on a serving platter.
- Season with salt and pepper.
- Add a drizzle of extra virgin olive oil and lemon zest.
- Serve and enjoy topped with Mediterranean salsa.

Cantaloupe and mozzarella Caprese salad

Ingredients

- 1 tablespoon of white balsamic vinegar
- 1 8- ounce of container mozzarella balls
- 10 slices of prosciutto shredded into large pieces
- Kosher salt and freshly ground black pepper
- 1 cantaloupe halved and seeded
- ¼ cup of mint leaves thinly sliced
- ¼ cup of basil leaves thinly sliced
- 3 tablespoons of extra-virgin olive oil
- 1 ½ tablespoons of honey

Directions

- Using a melon baller, scoop balls from the cantaloupe halves.
- Add to a large bowl.
- Add the mozzarella balls and the torn prosciutto.
- Sprinkle with the basil and mint leaves.

- In another small bowl, whisk the olive oil together with the honey and white balsamic vinegar.
- Season with kosher salt and freshly ground black pepper.
- Drizzle over the cantaloupe and toss.
- Season with more salt and pepper, herbs to taste.
- Serve and enjoy.

Tomato and hearts of palm salad

Ingredients

- 1 teaspoon of kosher salt
- 3 cups cherry tomatoes sliced in half
- ½ teaspoon of freshly ground black pepper
- 1 15- ounce can of hearts of palm drained and sliced.
- ¼ cup of vegetable oil
- 1 ½ tablespoon of red vinegar
- ¼ cup of thinly sliced
- 1 teaspoon of sugar
- ¼ cup of chopped Italian parsley

Directions

- Combine tomatoes together with the hearts of palm, red onion and parsley in a large bowl.
- In another small bowl, mix the vegetable oil with vinegar, sugar and salt and pepper until sugar is dissolved.
- Pour vinaigrette over tomato mixture and gently mix.
- Add more salt and pepper to taste.

- Serve and enjoy at room temperature.

Black bean and corn salad

This black bean and corn salad features poblano pepper, fresh mind and lime giving it a unique delicious taste.

Ingredients

- ½ tsp kosher salt
- 1 cup of cherry tomatoes, halved
- 2 ears corn, cleaned with no husks
- 1 ¾ cups of cooked black beans
- 1 tablespoon of extra virgin olive oil
- ½ cup of grated coconut from frozen
- ¼ cup of lightly packed mint leaves, chopped
- 2 tablespoons of fresh lime juice
- 1 medium poblano chili

Directions

- Wet two paper towels, squeeze out ant excess water.
- Wrap each ear of corn in the moist paper towel and place on a dinner plate.
- Cook in the microwave for 5 minutes.
- Let cool briefly then carefully remove the paper towel.

- Cut each cob in half crosswise, then stand one half at a time on a cutting board.
- Transfer the corn kernels to a large mixing bowl.
- Set the pablano pepper on the grates over a gas burner turned to high and use your tongs to turn the pepper until blackened in spots all over.
- Place roasted pablano in a bowl and cover plate, let steam for 10 minutes.
- Use your fingers to slip off the blackened skin, then remove and discard the stem and seeds.
- Chop the roasted pablano into ½-inch pieces and add to the mixing bowl with the corn.
- Add the black beans together with the coconut, lime juice, mint, tomatoes, olive oil and kosher salt. Toss.
- Taste and adjust accordingly.
- Serve and enjoy immediately.

Loaded Mediterranean chickpea salad

The manner in which the Mediterranean salad is loaded makes it a meal on its own for a Mediterranean Sea diet with a side of a perfectly roasted eggplant.

Ingredients

- Extra virgin olive oil.
- 3 tablespoons of Za'atar spice , divided
- 3 Roma tomatoes, diced
- 1 large lime, juice of
- ½ cucumber, diced
- 1 small red onion, sliced in ½ moons
- Salt and Pepper
- 1 cup cooked or canned chickpeas, drained
- 1 large eggplant, thinly sliced
- 1 cup of chopped parsley
- Salt
- 1 cup of chopped dill
- 2 garlic cloves, minced

Directions

- Place the sliced eggplant on a large tray and sprinkle generously with salt.

- Let it sit for 30 minutes to sweat out any bitterness.
- Line another large tray with a paper bag topped with paper towel and place it near the stove.
- Pat the eggplant dry.
- Then, heat 5 tablespoons of extra virgin olive oil over medium heat until shimmering but without smoke.
- Fry the eggplant in the oil in batches.
- Turn over the other side when the current ones turn golden brown.
- Remove the eggplant slices and arrange on paper towel-lined tray to drain and cool.
- Assemble the eggplant on a serving dish.
- Sprinkle with 1 tablespoon of Za'atar.
- In a medium mixing bowl, combine the tomatoes, cucumbers, chickpeas, red onions, parsley and dill.
- Add the remaining Za'atar, mix.
- In another small bowl, whisk together the dressing.

- Drizzle 2 tablespoons of salad dressing over the fried eggplant.
- Pour the remaining dressing over the chickpea salad and mix.
- Add the chickpea salad to the serving dish with the eggplant.
- Serve and enjoy

Mediterranean chickpea faro salad with shrimp

This is an easy to make satisfying salad it entails nutty faro parked with chopped vegetables and some herbs making it largely a vegetarian diet perfect for a Mediterranean Sea diet.

Ingredients

- 1 cucumber, diced
- ½ teaspoon of sumac
- 2 green onions, trimmed and chopped
- 2 ½ cup of cooked faro
- 1 large handful fresh parsley, chopped
- 15 mint leaves, chopped
- ½ teaspoon of ground cumin
- 1 lb. large shrimp, peeled and deveined
- Kosher salt
- Black pepper
- Extra virgin olive oil
- 2 cups of cooked chickpeas, drained and rinsed
- Juice of 1 lemon
- 10 oz. of cherry tomatoes, halved

- Black pepper
- 2 teaspoons of dried oregano

Directions

- In a small bowl, add the lemon, olive oil, salt, pepper, oregano, cumin, and sumac.
- Whisk well.
- In another large salad bowl, combine cooked faro together with the chickpeas and cherry tomatoes, cucumbers, green onion, parsley, and mint leaves.
- Pour the majority of the dressing on top of the salad, toss, set aside to let the flavors melt.
- Then, place uncooked shrimp in a bowl after patting dry with some paper towels.
- Season with salt and pepper.
- Drizzle extra virgin olive oil and toss to coat.
- Heat a skillet over high heat.
- Then, add shrimp and cook on one side till it starts to turn pink, turn over let cook 5 minutes.

- Turn off the heat then add the remaining 3 teaspoons of dressing to the hot shrimp, toss to coat.
- Shift to a serving platter. Make sure to add the shrimp on top.
- Serve and enjoy.

Avocado and Greek yogurt chicken salad

Ingredients

- 1/3 cup of chopped red onion
- 1/3 cup of chopped pecans
- 1 cup of plain yogurt
- 2 tablespoons of chopped fresh tarragon
- 1 avocado, mashed
- 1-2 tablespoons fresh lemon juice
- 1/3 cup of dried cranberries
- 2 cups of shredded chicken
- ¾ cup of chopped celery
- ½ cup of red grapes, halved
- Kosher salt and freshly ground black pepper

Directions

- In a small bowl, mix the yogurt with the avocado mash.
- Add lemon juice.
- Season with kosher salt and fresh ground pepper, keep aside.

- Add the shredded chicken to the chopped celery, grapes, pecans, red onion, tarragon and cranberries to a large bowl.
- Add the yogurt avocado sauce to the chicken mixture and toss until well combined
- Serve and enjoy as a sandwich or appetizer.

Lightning Source UK Ltd.
Milton Keynes UK
UKHW020644010621
384724UK00004B/46

9 781802 699050